A DK Publishing Book

Text Christopher Maynard
Project Editor Jane Donnelly
Designer Karen Lieberman
Deputy Managing Art Editor Jane Horne
Deputy Managing Editor Mary Ling
Production Ruth Cobb
Consultant Theresa Greenaway
Picture Researcher Tom Worsley

Additional photography by Dave King, Cyril Laubscher, Tim Ridley, Paul Bricknell, Susannah Price, Steve Gorton, Philip Dowell

First American Edition, 1997
2 4 6 8 10 9 7 5 3 1

Published in the United States by DK Publishing, Inc.,
95 Madison Avenue, New York, New York 10016
Visit us on the World Wide Web at http://www.dk.com

Copyright © 1997 Dorling Kindersley Limited, London

Published in Great Britain by Dorling Kindersley Ltd.

A CIP catalog record for this book is available
from the Library of Congress.

ISBN: 0-7894-1529-1

Color reproduction by Chromagraphics, Singapore
Printed and bound in Italy by L.E.G.O.

The publisher would like to thank the following for their kind permission to reproduce their photographs:
t top, b bottom, l left, r right, c center, BC back cover, FC front cover
Bruce Coleman Collection: (Why is it dark...?)c; **Robert Harding Picture Library**: (Why do seasons...?)cr, br, cl, bl, (Why do we use sundials...?)c; **Image Bank**: Frank Whitney (Why does the Moon...?)br; **Tony Stone Images**: Geoff Dore (Why does the Moon...?)c, Mark Lewis (Why do seasons...?)br, JF Preedy (Why do birds...?)br, James Randklev (Why are baby birds...?)br, Paul Rees (Why do birds...?)bl, Jerome Tisne (Why do I only...?)c, BC cb, Mark Wagner (Why does the time...?)c, John Warden (Why do birds...?)c; **Telegraph Colour Library**: FC cb, (Why do I only...?)bl, (Why are baby birds...?)c, Endpapers

Questions

Why do seasons change?

Why do birds migrate?

Why is it dark at night?

Why does the Moon change shape?

Why do I only have one birthday a year?

Why are baby birds born in spring?

Why does the time change when we travel?

Why do we use sundials?

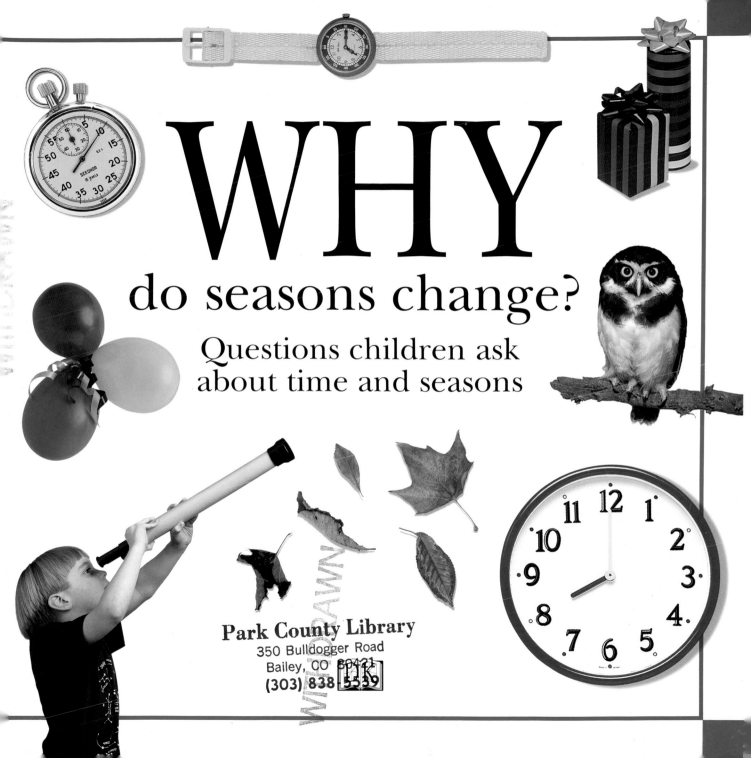

WHY

do seasons change?

Questions children ask about time and seasons

Seasons change because the Earth tilts. The north leans toward the sun and has summer, while the south leans away and has winter.

Why is it cold in winter?
As the Earth circles the sun, the part leaning away from its hot rays has cold, winter weather.

change?

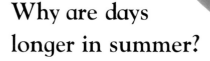

Why are days longer in summer?
In summer, the sun climbs very high in the sky. So on summer evenings, it takes longer for the sun to dip down below the horizon. In winter, the sun rises lower in the sky and this makes the days much shorter.

Why do birds

As the days get shorter and colder in winter, many birds fly away, or migrate, to go to places where the weather is warmer and where there is plenty of food to be found.

Why are trees bare in winter?
Snow and strong winds would damage a tree's leaves. So trees

migrate?

Why do some animals sleep in winter? Sleeping deeply all winter is called hibernation. Animals store fat in their bodies before they hibernate. In this way they survive the cold months when there is little food.

stop sending water to their leaves and withdraw useful chemicals from them. The leaves then fall off.

Why is it dark

Earth spins like a giant top. When one side faces the sun it has daytime. The side facing away from the sun is dark and has nighttime.

Why is it hottest at midday?
By midday, the sun has been warming the Earth for hours, and it is still high in the sky, giving its

at night?

Why do we have shadows?
Sunlight travels in
straight lines. When
it shines on one
side of you,
your body blocks
the light, casting
a pool of shade that
shows your outline.

full heat to the Earth. Once the
sun begins to sink, the effect of its
rays diminishes, and the air cools.

Why does the Moon change

The Moon shines because it reflects sunlight. As the Moon travels around the Earth, we see different amounts of its sunlit face because the Earth casts a shadow on it. In a full Moon, light is reflected off the whole, round face of the Moon.

Why is the Moon so bright?
The Moon has no light of its own. However, sometimes it reflects the

shape?

Why is the Moon sometimes out in the day? The Moon may be out anytime, day or night. But in broad daylight, the sky is far too bright to see it. Later in the day, as sunshine fades, the Moon comes into view again.

sun's light so brightly that you can see well enough to read a book outdoors at midnight!

Why do I only have

Birthdays celebrate the day you were born. This date only comes around once a year. If you've just had a birthday, you'll have to wait a year for the next!

Why is a year so long?
A year measures the time it takes the Earth to go once around the sun,

one birthday a year?

Why do people get older?
Time can only go forward. Every minute that passes, we all get a little bit older. The more time goes by, the older we get. You can see how people change if you look at photographs taken years apart.

which is just over 365 days. A year is always the same because the Earth moves at the same speed.

Why are baby

Spring is when the weather warms up and new plants and grass start to grow. Baby animals have a much better chance of surviving then than if they are born in the winter.

Why does some fruit ripen in the fall?
It takes a whole summer of sunshine for some plants to produce fruit. It is not until

birds born in spring?

Why do some flowers close their petals at night?
Some flowers shut their petals as the sun sets to protect themselves from the cool night air and from being attacked by nighttime creatures. These flowers wait for the hot sunshine to open up again.

he fall that the fruit is fully grown. Tropical fruits ripen all year round – here is no fall in the tropics.

Why does the time

Earth is always turning, so the sun begins to light up each part of it at a different time. People set their clocks according to this time. If we travel by jet, we may land in places with different local times.

Why does a plane move so slowly across the sky?
When it flies low over your house, a jet comes and goes in a flash. But high in the sky, it takes several

change when we travel?

Why does jet lag make you sleepy?
The world is divided into regions called time zones. Jet lag happens when you arrive in a time zone several hours ahead or behind your own. It may be morning, but it's the middle of the night at home.

minutes to pass by. This is because it is far enough away for you to see it fly 15 or 20 miles before it is out of your sight.

Sundials measure the shadow cast by the sun as it moves across the sky. The shadow changes each hour.

Why do clocks have twelve numbers?
There are 24 hours in every day. We count the first half of the day up to 12 noon, and then start again and count to 12 midnight.

sundials?

Why do clocks have two hands?

The long hand moves steadily to mark off minutes. The short hand moves 12 times slower to mark off each hour. Some clocks have a third hand to mark seconds.